CALIFORNIA

THE AMERICAN FOOD LIBRARY

A Guide to Regional Foods

CALIFORNIA

written by

Janet Greenberg

Rourke Publications, Inc.

The following sources are acknowledged and thanked for the use of their color transparencies in this work:
Janet Greenberg p. 7; Pasadena Tournament of Roses p. 18; Ivor Markman pp. 2, 8, 10, 11, 13, 14, 17, 19, 20, 21, 22, 23, 24, 25, 26, 27, 28, 29, 32, 34, 46; Paul O'Connor pp. 36, 39, 41, 43.
Cover photograph by Ivor Markman.
Food styling by David Hundley and Nancy Diamond.

Produced by Salem Press, Inc.

∞ The paper used in this book conforms to the American National Standard for Permanence of Paper for Printed Library Materials, Z39.48-1984.

Library of Congress Cataloging-in-Publication Data
Greenberg, Janet, 1955-
    California / Janet Greenberg.
        p.   cm. — (The American food library)
    Includes index.
    ISBN 0-86625-511-7
    1. Cookery, American—California style—Juvenile literature.   2. California—Description and travel—Juvenile literature.   [1. Cookery, American—California style.   2. California.]   I. Title.   II. Series.
TX715.2.C34G74   1994
641.59794—dc20   94-1038
                                                                           CIP
                                                                           AC

First Printing

PRINTED IN THE UNITED STATES OF AMERICA

Contents

1

AN INTRODUCTION
TO CALIFORNIA

Sitting on the western edge of the continent, California enjoys a unique geography and history. Bordered on the west by the Pacific Ocean, on the south by Mexico, on the north by Oregon, and on the east by the spine of the great Sierra Nevada and the wide flowing Colorado River, California is larger than some European countries and is the third largest state following Texas and Alaska.

The coastal region in the west lies between the mountains of the Coast Range and the Pacific Ocean, the area that drew the first settlers and explorers to California. The southern third of the state, from Santa Barbara to the Mexican border, is mostly desert. A large part of the rest of the state is a fertile agricultural valley, the San Joaquin and the Sacramento Valleys, bordered to the east by the mighty Sierra Nevada and the west by the Coast Range.

The diversity of geography is so great that before Alaska became a state, California boasted both the highest and the lowest points of land in the United States, Mount Whitney and Death Valley. This diversity also allows people in Southern California to go water skiing in the ocean on Christmas Day while those living in the Sierras go snow skiing in the mountains.

The first Spanish explorers arrived in California by ship and settled on the coast. These original settlements grew into California's port cities: Los Angeles, the largest of California's cities with a population of almost 3,000,000 people; San Diego,

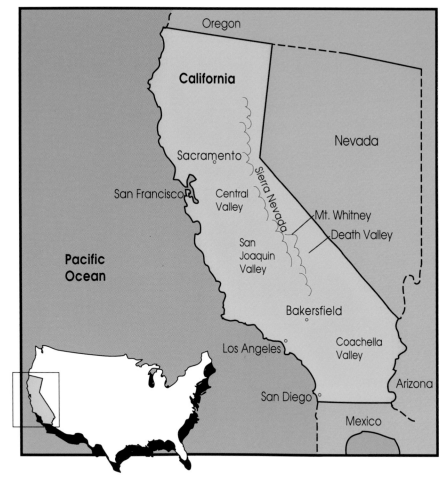

home to nearly 1,000,000 inhabitants; and San Francisco, with some 700,000 residents. These Spanish explorers also contributed much to California's cultural heritage. Many places in California carry the Spanish names which the early settlers gave them, such as Los Angeles, "the city of angels"; Salinas, "the place of salt marshes"; and Sierra Nevada, "snowy mountains."

When the first Spanish explorers arrived, they brought with them horses, plants, and their religion. The Native Americans they encountered had never seen horses or these new plants, and they already had a religion of their own which was very different from Christianity. Missionaries founded missions to teach the Indians about Christianity. Led by Father

Junipero Serra, the missionaries settled communities along the coast from Mission San Diego in the south to Mission San Francisco Solano in the north. These missions became the centers of life in early Spanish California.

The geography of California dictated where the new settlers would live and what crops and animals they could raise. The dry desert areas in the south were very good for growing oranges and other citrus fruit, but they were not good for growing grapes and wheat or raising cattle. The Central Valley of California, a fertile place where a wide variety of plants could be grown throughout the year, was planted with wheat, onions, peaches, plums, apricots, berries, and greens brought by the growing European population. The area north of San Francisco was the best area for growing grapes. Beef, and later goats and lambs, grazed in the green foothills bordering the San Joaquin Valley and well into the Sacramento Valley. Farms continued to pop up wherever there was water, and in Central and Northern California there were many rivers to feed the fields of crops.

Soon more people were attracted to the West Coast. They came to buy land, to become part of the growing trade, to enjoy the gentle climate, and to get rich! The discovery of gold in 1848 and the Gold Rush that followed was the biggest boost to the growth and development of California in the history of the state. The miners needed supplies, food, and transportation. Shops that sold clothing and provisions flourished. Roads and railroads were built. As news of the big strike at Sutter's Mill circled the world, people from many exotic places began to arrive in California by the thousands.

With the completion of the transcontinental railroad, it became easier for people from the eastern United States and Europe to reach California. In 1915, the opening of the Panama Canal again improved travel to the West Coast, and California became a more important center of trade. As communications and transportation improved, more people from across the Pacific entered California. The Chinese were the earliest Asian settlers, but later they were joined by Japanese, Vietnamese, Laotians, Cambodians, and Koreans. Whether they came to escape the hard life in their own countries or to seek the golden sunshine of California, as long as there was land, people continued to come. This fabric of Hispanic, European, and Asian cultures produced the mixtures of unique foods that the world has come to call "California Cuisine."

The Hmong are one of the more recent Asian people to settle in California in large numbers. Here, they celebrate their heritage in Sacramento.

2

HISTORICAL BACKGROUND

Mission San Juan Capistrano continues to attract visitors every year when the swallows return to nest there.

Although both California and Mexico were part of New Spain, it took nearly two hundred years for Spain to commission Father Junipero Serra and Juan de Portola to settle *Alta California*. Father Serra began building missions near the coast along the *El Camino Real*, the Royal Road. Each mission was located within one day's journey from the next so the Spanish pioneers would never be too far from food, shelter, or a place to pray. The missions were both places of worship and centers in which the Span-

iards and new converts gathered in a community. The first mission was built in 1769 in San Diego and the last in 1823 in what is now Sonoma County.

The Native Americans provided the labor that built the missions. In return, they received shelter, food, and a place to practice their new religion. They learned to grow crops instead of relying on nature for their food, and they slowly gave up their native culture in the hope that the Spaniards would offer them a better and easier way of life. Instead, the Spaniards and later the Mexicans enslaved the Indians and denied them equal privileges. Many of the Indians became sick and died from diseases the Spanish brought with them. By the time the last mission was built, the Indian population was only half of what it had been when the first missionaries arrived.

By 1810, the people of New Spain had grown tired of being controlled by Spain, and they revolted. The Indians and Spanish Mexicans who lived in what we now know as Mexico won the War of Independence, but the people of *Alta California* did not even know about the war until it was over. Many changes now lay in store for them. The Russians were allowed to hunt seals and otter at Fort Ross and trade the furs to the missionaries in exchange for food. Spain no longer sent supplies to the West Coast, so soon England and the United States filled the gap left by the Spanish.

With trade came new settlers from Europe and the United States. The Mexican government began to worry that the new settlers would want independence from Mexico, and their fears were well founded. In 1846, California won its independence from Mexico, and four years later it became the thirty-first state of the United States of America.

In 1848, gold was discovered in California, and the following year gold seekers, nicknamed Forty-niners, came from as far away as Europe and Asia to strike it rich. Gradually many of the miners had

The Gold Rush did not make every miner a millionaire. However, the deserted mines and towns are now famous with tourists.

to accept that they would not get rich from gold, and they recognized the need for tradesmen and farmers that the growing population had created.

At the same time, many Chinese miners found that they could grow vegetables on their claim and make more money selling the food than by mining for gold. Their presence was strengthened when thousands of Chinese were brought to California to work on the transcontinental railroad. Some became cooks in the lumber and mining camps, and some even went on to open restaurants. They introduced such vegetables as water chestnuts and snow peas and such new ways of cooking as stir fry, cooking vegetables quickly to preserve the flavor and color. This was to be a lasting contribution to California cooking.

The completion of the transcontinental railroad in 1869 opened California to more immigrants from Europe. The Italians took up raising grapes and making wine, as they had done for centuries in Italy. They also introduced new vegetables such as broccoli, zucchini, and artichokes. Thanks to these early immigrants California gained a worldwide reputation as a wine-producing region and as a source of abundant year-round produce.

With the twentieth century came improved irrigation technology, which brought water to the dry interior of California. Farms sprang up where there had been only desert, making more land available to newcomers. The Los Angeles Aqueduct took water away from farmers in the Owens Valley and channeled it 250 miles to the south, allowing the city of Los Angeles to grow and spread into the metropolis it is today.

The Los Angeles Aqueduct steals water from the Owens Valley and channels it some 250 miles to metropolitan Los Angeles.

With water, people could settle in new regions, and more people came to California. Many industries took advantage of these new workers and flourished. At first it was farming, then mining for oil and gas, and then the budding moving picture industry that drew the attention of the world to California. More people chose to search for their dreams in California, where land was plentiful, opportunities abundant, and the weather gentle.

3

SPECIAL EVENTS
IN CALIFORNIA

Because the history of California was shaped so strongly by the Spaniards and Mexicans, Californians observe many holidays that are not celebrated in many parts of the United States. In fact, many of the events in California owe much to the various immigrant groups who came to settle the West Coast. Chinese New Year is a big event in Los Angeles, Monterey, and San Francisco. *Cinco de Mayo* is celebrated all over Southern California. As a result of the mixture of cultures, many traditional holidays such as Christmas, Easter, and Thanksgiving are celebrated with a slightly unexpected flair in California.

Cinco de Mayo, the Fifth of May, is celebrated with parades and fiestas all over the state but with special enthusiasm in the southern cities of Los Angeles and San Diego. This holiday celebrates Mexico's independence from French occupation on May 5, 1862. On Olvera Street, the original center of Los Angeles, people dance, play music, and some even dress as Mexican Revolutionaries.

In the early spring, the cities of Los Angeles and San Francisco explode with the excitement of Chinese New Year. The ancient Chinese calendar differs for our Western calendar, and each of the Chinese years is associated with an animal, for example the Year of the Dragon. The celebration lasts for a week and includes fireworks and parades with shimmering, long dragons and beautiful costumes. There are also many traditional foods that are only eaten during the New Year celebration. One such food is a

baked fish. The head and tail are considered delicacies and are the most prized morsels. The whole fish is a symbol of completion and beginning. A breakfast food is a sweet noodle that takes a lot of time to prepare. It is a symbol of the sweetness hoped for in the New Year.

All over California people look forward to the many open air events that take place during the summer. In Southern California, the opening of the Hollywood Bowl brings people to this outdoor amphitheater to listen to the Los Angeles Philharmonic Orchestra. The picnics the music lovers bring with them are almost as important as the performance they will hear.

San Diego is host to the world famous Shakespeare Festival at the Old Globe Theatre in beautiful Balboa Park. The high quality of the performances and the lovely California summer evenings draw theatergoers from all over the country as well as the rest of the world.

There are two events in California that the rest of the world joins on television. The first festival to take place in California each year is the Tournament of Roses Parade. On January 1, large floats decorated entirely with roses and other flowers travel the wide boulevards of Pasadena. The day's events lead to the Rose Bowl where a championship college football game is played each year. The "Rose Parade" shows the rest of the world how beautiful and warm California is even on New Year's Day. It is one of the most famous parades in the world.

New Year's Day focuses the country's attention on the Rose Bowl in Pasadena.

The second event watched by television viewers the world round is the annual Academy Awards presentation. These awards given to technicians and artists in the movie industry bring out the stars and stargazers alike. Many people have parties where they can guess who will win which award and talk about what the stars are wearing. All in all, it is another good reason to have a party!

Although not many are famous, festivals abound in California. One could go to some kind of festival, be it music, art, or food, every single weekend of the year. From the world renowned Monterey Jazz Festival in June to the Ojai "Bowlful of Blues" festival, there is an event for every interest and every culture. In July, the World Championship Rodeo in Salinas attracts cowboys and cowgirls from all fifty states. In June and July the many Japanese communities in California celebrate the traditional Lotus Blossom Festival.

Garlic lovers gather in the central California town

The State Fair in Sacramento draws fun lovers to both the exhibits and amusement park.

of Gilroy for the annual Garlic Harvest and Festival. There are recipe contests, games, and music written to celebrate the local food known as the "Stinking Rose." Among the other events in California based on local agriculture or food is the Butter and Egg Days, celebrated in Petaluma in April. Once known as the "Egg Basket" of the country, Petaluma residents continue to celebrate their heritage with parades, antique shows, and reenactments of historical moments in their history as a rich dairy center.

4

AGRICULTURE IN CALIFORNIA

Picking lettuce in the Coachella Valley still is done by hand and requires many farm laborers.

If you go into the produce section of your local supermarket, chances are you will see many of the vegetables and fruits that are grown on California farms. California produces most of the kiwi fruit, tomatoes, lettuce, table grapes, prunes, almonds, walnuts, figs, dates, nectarines, apricots, broccoli, asparagus, and carrots delivered to stores nationwide. The wide ranging climate and available water allow Californians to grow this great variety of produce. In fact, there are more than two hundred crops grown in the "Golden State."

The great Central Valley enjoys water from the Sacramento and San Joaquin Rivers and is bordered on the east and west by the Sierra Nevada and the Coast Range. The rich soil came down from the mountain ranges full of minerals, and the two biggest crops in California, lettuce and tomatoes, are grown here. You could call this valley "America's Salad Bowl." Also grown in the Central Valley are wheat, rice, almonds, plums, olives, and livestock for meat and dairy farming.

Northwest of the Central Valley lie Napa and Sonoma counties, which are best known for producing wine. As people from Europe immigrated to this area north of San Francisco, they brought with them knowledge of vineyards and cuttings from the many varieties of wine grapes that had never been grown outside their native countries. By 1900, California was already producing 80 percent of the wine produced in the United States.

A little south of the Central Valley is the city and county of Fresno. This county produces more crops than any county in the other forty-nine states. The major crops from this area are lettuce, broccoli, potatoes, cantaloupes, and strawberries. In the far south, the Coachella Valley has been turned into a rich agricultural area through the introduction of water. What was once a desert is now home to citrus groves, date groves, and fields of crops which thrive in a warm climate.

The largest part of California's agricultural income comes from livestock. Milk is the state's number one agricultural product. Then follow, in order of importance, beef, eggs, sheep, and turkeys. Today, most of the livestock is raised in the southern part of the Central Valley, in the mild Fresno and Imperial counties. It also helps that these areas produce the state's largest feed crops, including hay, alfalfa, barley, and corn.

Though the produce that comes to our markets from California looks plump, beautiful, and tasty, it

wasn't always that way. Many agricultural advances have taken place since the 1700's when the first Franciscan missionaries planted their twigs of wine grapes and their orange trees. Experimentation with crops began when the Forty-niners, who came in the Gold Rush, flooded the state in search of gold. Suddenly there were many people to feed. Many of the Forty-niners brought cattle from the East with them. These cattle were heartier and better suited for breeding than the ones the Spanish and Mexicans had bred.

In fact, the Gold Rush was a great boost to the agriculture of the state. Here are some figures to show the rapid agricultural growth during and after the Gold Rush:

	1850	1860
Cattle	262,000 head	1,180,000 head
Butter	707 pounds	3,095,035 pounds

Until 1917, the annual vegetable crop was valued at four times the value of gold mined in California.

Some credit for the high quality and large production of California produce goes to the state's universities, where professors investigate how to make tomatoes resistant to certain diseases, or how to use the soil without draining it of all its vitamins, and even how to use friendly bugs to control pests instead of using pesticides!

Because of the state's moderate climate, crops that only grow in the spring in other parts of the country grow here year round. Valencia orange groves take advantage of the climate, strawberries can be grown through the end of summer in California, and tomatoes of one variety or another can be grown all year round. This extended growing season makes California produce very attractive to people in other countries, who enjoy much of California's bounty throughout the year as well. In fact, a full one third of the state's agricultural products are exported.

Oranges from California are probably as well known worldwide as those from Florida.

5

FOOD CUSTOMS
IN CALIFORNIA

All over the world, people refer to a certain kind of cooking as "California Cuisine," or California cooking. What they are really referring to is a style of cooking that combines many ethnic foods and cooking methods in fresh, new ways. California cooking is a casual blend of many different kinds of foods and styles of cooking rather than a single formal approach to cooking. In California, anything goes!

During the early years of colonization and for some time thereafter, much of the food prepared in California was based on the cuisine of Mexico, California's nearest neighbor and closest relative. Many dishes developed from very traditional Mexican cooking. Tamale Pie is a casserole made with tamales, corn, and chili. Gazpacho, a cold soup made of tomatoes, bell peppers, celery, and onion, has its origin in Mexican cooking.

We owe a great deal of thanks to the many immigrants who brought different foods to California. We also thank them for giving us many ways to prepare those foods. The Chinese immigrants taught us to cook foods over a very hot fire and to cook them very fast. Perhaps you have heard of "stir fry." This method of cooking in a shallow pan called a wok allows foods to cook fast enough so that they keep their individual flavors and textures, unlike stewing in which many flavors blend as foods are cooked together slowly for a long time. Stir-fry style cooking has greatly influenced the way Californians cook today.

Miners had a short time in which to strike it rich. This log cabin is typical of the quickly constructed homes they built for themselves.

It is easy to talk about "stir fry" as a popular method of cooking in California today, but early Californians experienced a very different way of cooking. Green vegetables were hard to find or inconvenient to carry inland on horseback, and they were almost nonexistent in the gold mining camps. What those early miners, trappers, and explorers contributed to California cuisine is outdoor cooking. Everything was once cooked over an open flame, either on a spit or simmered in a pot over the fire for a long time. These people had learned that you could put a variety of ingredients into one pot, cook them all together, and end up with a hearty meal. One of these all-in-one-pot meals was labelled the "Hangtown Fry," named after the lawless gold mining town of Hangtown in which it first became popular. It included beef, lard, potatoes, eggs, and just about anything else that was on hand.

Some might say that the popularity of barbecuing

in California began with the miners of the 1840's. Californians cook just about everything on a barbecue. Fish, steaks, hamburgers, chicken, turkey, and vegetables all are grilled. Different kinds of wood are used as fuel to give very different flavors to the foods being cooked. In the southern part of the state mesquite is often used, whereas in Northern California grape vines are preferred! The Mexicans, Portuguese, Italians, and Japanese each introduced us to their own form of barbecue. Whether you call it a hibachi, a robata, or a barbecue, it is truly a tradition shared by many cultures.

As trade with the Far East became more open and free, California also was introduced to foods and cooking methods from Japan. Combinations of very delicate flavors and both raw fish, called sushi or sashimi, and slightly cooked fish became popular. Before the popularity of Japanese food, few people in California had tasted fresh tuna. Most people only

The fishing industry is important to California and has grown with the popularity of Asian cooking and an increased demand for fish as a healthy alternative to beef, pork, and lamb.

were familiar with the small cans of tuna we usually mix with mayonnaise to make tuna salad. Now fresh tuna can be purchased in many parts of the country.

Not long ago, people thought of California food as "health" food, with bean sprouts and alfalfa sprouts in every dish. In fact, Californians do tend to eat healthier than people in many other states. With a long growing season and so many fresh foods available locally, they can get their food from farm to table in a short amount of time with few preservatives. In the past ten years, Californians have become ever more inventive with vegetables, thanks in part to the chefs who have tried some very interesting combinations.

Tomatoes are common to many Mexican dishes and most salads, and the California harvest is a plentiful one.

Another California custom is to serve salads as a main course rather than simply as a side dish. The more traditional salads begin with lettuce, but a Mexican salad, a *tostada*, begins with a tortilla, and then beans, lettuce, and salsa are heaped on top. The Italians brought with them a salad of many grilled vegetables called *antipasto*. Today one can find a salad made only of vegetables or a salad made with beef or chicken and just a bit of vegetables. The fact remains that wherever there are a few raw leafy vegetables and any leftovers, Californians will throw them together and invent a new salad.

As the people of California develop a taste for unusual foods from far away places, the demand increases on farmers and ranchers to grow these exotic foods in California. The more things California grows, the more the rest of the country becomes curious to try them.

6

FOOD TRADITIONS IN CALIFORNIA

California is like a small country with a variety of geographies and foods available in different places throughout the state. In the Southern part of the state where the climate is sunny and the landscape desertlike, the strongest influence on food is Mexican. The available ingredients include lots of citrus fruit, onions, peppers, corn, and plenty of fish. Dishes baked with tomatoes such as Halibut Veracruz or tamales made from fresh corn are easy to find in Southern California. Drinks made from fresh fruit—such as fresh squeezed orange juice—and even drinks made with fresh watermelon are also popular here.

As you would expect, the coastal region celebrates its relationship to the state's biggest food supplier—the sea. From San Diego to Mendocino and as far north as Klamath, fish and seafood remain the centerpiece of local cooking. San Diegans love to barbecue fresh swordfish with a little bit of salt and lime juice, and they even turn it into fish tacos by stuffing a warm tortilla with chunks of fish and a little fresh salsa. Close to the Russian River—about an hour north of San Francisco—salmon is the prize catch, and here people cure the salmon with lemon. Still others throw it on the grill and relish the resulting taste. Along the central coast, the abalone is among the rarest and most prized treasures of the sea. Sometimes it costs up to $35.00 per pound, and people sauté it in butter and simply savor the natural flavor.

The Napa and Sonoma Valleys are heavily influ-

enced by French and Italian traditions in cooking. These are the areas of the greatest wine production in the state, and many of the vintners brought not only grapes but also a style of cooking with them to California. They also planted olive groves, and olive oil has had a major impact in this area as a source of agricultural income and also as a basis of great cooking. As in their native countries of France and Italy, people in this part of California celebrate the grape harvest in the fall with parties and celebrations. They make paté and fresh cheeses to enjoy with their wine. Fresh breads and casseroles of beef and olives not only are welcome on a cool autumn evening but also complement the new wines. A variety of vegetables grilled the Italian way—charred over an open flame, then slowly roasted—are another traditional way these Northern Californians celebrate the bounty of the fall harvest.

In and around Sacramento and throughout the San Joaquin Valley people pride themselves on home cooking. With a small town feeling, many of the cities in the Central Valley—Sacramento, Stockton, Visalia, and Fresno—have cooking contests to celebrate their local fare—onions, lettuce, squash, and plenty of beef and dairy products. Often, the local rodeo is accompanied by a chili cook-off, attracting cowboys and city folks alike. A typical California chili starts with onions, beef, beans, and tomato sauce. The variations are endless and they tend to reflect the flavors available locally. A chili stew in Gilroy might be filled with garlic cloves and have no onions at all, whereas a chili in Napa might be made with chicken and white beans.

Some of the best chili you will ever taste is served at the Salinas Rodeo and Chili Cook-off each July. The smells that float through the dusty summer heat will hit you first, but the day will end with that hearty meal-in-a-pot of ground beef, onions, green peppers, tomatoes, and red beans that is guaranteed to taste better than anything you could imagine.

The French and Italian settlers in the Napa and Sonoma Valleys brought their tradition of olive oil production with them to California and planted olive groves.

In San Francisco, Chinese cooking has had a great influence on what people actually cook at home. This is partly a result of the fact that San Francisco has the largest Chinese population outside of China. In addition, the techniques of Chinese cooking lend themselves well to the diverse fresh foods available in California. Stir fry is a great way to prepare almost any food, whether asparagus, green chilis, beef, or shrimp. The idea is like that of chili, where only one pot is used, but unlike slow-cooking chili, stir fry cooks quickly so each food retains its own flavor.

Rice, an ingredient so common to Chinese cooking, is grown in the nearby Sacramento Valley. This and other ingredients associated with ethnic cuisine become uniquely Californian when cooks mix a variety of them from various ethnic cuisines. Where but in California would a cook dare to put pea pods

The Chinese population in San Francisco has left its mark not only on the architecture of San Francisco but also on its cuisine.

and mushrooms over pasta or serve fried rice cakes with Mexican black bean sauce. Sometimes it is just a little twist in a traditional recipe that makes it taste new and different. If you are used to having ketchup on your hamburger, why not try salsa? Or if you are making a traditional lasagna, try adding spinach instead of eggplant, or eggplant instead of beef. The list of ingredients you can experiment with increases as you become familiar with the tastes available in your kitchen. California cooking encourages you to try mixing things up. So when you cook, think about how they might do it in California.

Brunch in Mendocino

Scrambled Eggs with Salmon
Tomato and Avocado Salsa

Scrambled Eggs with Salmon

> *6 eggs*
> *¼ cup milk*
> *1 scallion, sliced thin up to the light green stalk*
> *4 oz. fresh Salmon filet, cut into small pieces*
> *1 teaspoon fresh dill or ¼ teaspoon dried dill*
> *1 tablespoon butter*

**Scrambled Eggs
with Salmon**

Note: Each recipe serves four, unless otherwise stated.

1. Beat eggs together with milk and dill in a bowl. Set aside.
2. Put butter and scallions in a sauté pan and turn heat to medium high.
3. When the scallions begin to get soft, add salmon and cook for about 12 minutes.
4. Add beaten egg mixture and turn down heat to medium.
5. Stir with wooden spoon to prevent egg from burning or sticking.
6. Turn off heat while eggs are still moist looking. They will continue to cook.
7. Add salt and pepper. Serve with tomato and avocado salsa.

Tomato and Avocado Salsa

4 medium tomatoes or 8 small Roma tomatoes
1 avocado
$\frac{1}{4}$ cup jicama
2 scallions
2 radishes
salt and pepper
1 teaspoon lemon juice

1. Dice the tomatoes.
2. Cut a piece of jicama and cut away the tough skin. Cut the inside into sticks, then chop.
3. Chop scallions (white part only) and radishes.
4. Mix all of the ingredients with a little lemon juice, salt, and pepper.
5. Peel, thinly slice, then cube the avocado. Carefully mix into salsa. Serve on the side with scrambled eggs.

Everyday Lunch

Gazpacho
Championship Chili
Tortillas

Gazpacho *(Cold, Crunchy Vegetable Soup)*
  4 tablespoons olive oil
  1 cup beef broth
  3 cups tomato juice
  2 scallions
  1 large tomato
  2 stalks celery
  1 large bell pepper
  juice of $\frac{1}{2}$ lemon
  1 cucumber
  $\frac{1}{2}$ cup sour cream
  $\frac{1}{4}$ teaspoon Worcestershire sauce

  1. Chop vegetables into small pieces.
  2. Mix the liquids with oil in the blender.
  3. Add the vegetables to the liquid and chill in the refrigerator for 1 hour.
  4. Serve with warm tortillas and a spoonful of sour cream on the top of each bowl of soup.

Championship Chili
  oil
  3 medium onions, finely chopped
  2 medium green peppers, finely chopped
  8 lbs. coarsely ground beef
  1 can (6 oz.) tomato paste
  2 cans (1 lb., 12 oz.) stewed tomatoes
  2 cans (16 oz.) tomato sauce
  3 cloves garlic, finely chopped
  2 jars (3 oz.) chili powder
  2 tablespoons salt
  oregano
  1 can (7 oz.) chili salsa

1 medium jalepeno chili, seeded and chopped
   (optional)
garlic salt
coarsely ground black pepper

1. Brush bottom of heavy two-gallon pot with oil.
2. Sauté onions, green peppers, and celery for 10 minutes.
3. Add meat and cook for another 10 to 15 minutes, or until meat loses its pink color.
4. Stir in tomato paste, stewed tomatoes, and tomato sauce.
5. Add chopped garlic, chili powder, salt, a sprinkling of oregano, chili salsa, and jalapeno chili. Simmer for 30 minutes.
6. Season to taste with garlic salt and pepper, then simmer $2\frac{1}{2}$ hours, stirring every 10-15 minutes.
7. Skim off fat occasionally. Makes about 2 gallons. Plenty to freeze! Serve with grated cheese sprinkled on top. Serve with plenty of cold soda and fresh bread or tortillas.

Championship Chili

Everyday Meal

Cartwheel Salad
Tamale Pie

Cartwheel Salad

1 head iceberg lettuce
1 green pepper, chopped
2 large tomatoes, diced
2 cups tortilla chips, crumbled
1 can sliced olives
1 small can julienne beets
1 avocado, sliced
1 hard cooked egg, chopped

1. Tear lettuce into bite-sized pieces and put into round salad bowl.
2. Place the above ingredients in pie shaped sections, extending out from the center, on top of the lettuce. One section of green pepper, then tomatoes, avocado, and so on until all sections are covered with a topping. Do not toss or serve this until everyone gets a chance to see the design.

Dressing

1 package of Italian salad dressing mix
2 tablespoons water
2 tablespoons chopped green pepper
2 tablespoons chopped pickled beets
2 tablespoons hard cooked egg
$\frac{1}{4}$ cup vinegar
$\frac{2}{3}$ cup salad oil

1. In a tight sealing container, combine all ingredients except oil, put on lid, and shake to mix thoroughly.

Cartwheel Salad

2. Add oil, shake again. Chill before serving.
3. Pour over salad when ready to serve and mix with salad fork and spoon. Makes $1\frac{1}{2}$ cups.

Tamale Pie

4 large XLNT brand tamales
1 can chili con carne
1 pound sharp yellow cheese, grated
1 can (10 oz.) niblet corn
1 can (10 oz.) creamed corn
1 can (7 oz.) sliced olives

1. Slice the tamales and line the bottom of Pyrex casserole.
2. Mix half the olives with the rest of the ingredients except the cheese.
3. Put this mixture on top of the tamales, cover with cheese, and sprinkle the other olives on top as a decoration.
4. Bake at 350 degrees for 45 minutes.

A Festive Meal in the Wine Country

Braised Beef with Olives
Garlic Mashed Potatoes
Steamed Onions and Carrots
Blushing Pears

Braised Beef with Olives

4 strips bacon, diced
1 large onion, chopped
2 pounds beef stew meat, cut in small cubes
flour
1 cup California Burgundy or other red wine
1 can (8 oz.) tomato sauce
1 bay leaf, crumbled
$^1/_4$ teaspoon each: thyme, marjoram, salt, pepper
1 cup ripe pitted olives, halved
2 tablespoons chopped parsley

1. Cook bacon and onion together slowly in a Dutch oven or other heavy kettle until light brown.
2. Dredge meat in flour, add to kettle, and brown slowly on all sides. (If bacon is lean, 1 to 2 tablespoons of shortening may be added to brown the meat.)
3. Add wine, tomato sauce, and seasonings.
4. Cover and cook gently for about 2 hours, or until meat is tender.
5. Stir frequently and add water as needed during cooking to keep gravy from becoming too thick.
6. Shortly before serving add olives and parsley. Serve with steamed onions and carrots and garlic mashed potatoes.

Garlic Mashed Potatoes

2 garlic bulbs
olive oil
5 baking potatoes, peeled
milk
salt and pepper

1. Cut tops (not the root end) off garlic to expose tops of cloves, leaving all the other skin on.
2. Rub with a little olive oil and place on foil in 250 degree oven for $1\frac{1}{2}$ hours, or until cloves start to push up and out of their casing.
3. Cover peeled potatoes with water in a large pot and turn the heat to boil. Boil the potatoes until tender (test with a fork). Drain water and begin to mash them with masher in the bottom of the pot.

Garlic Mashed Potatoes

4. At the same time, squeeze the garlic bulbs to release the soft cloves onto a plate. Mash them with the back of a fork, then place them into the pot with the potatoes.
5. Mix the garlic in, then add milk little by little until the potatoes are the right consistency for your taste. Salt and pepper to taste.

Steamed or Boiled Onions and Carrots

12 small white onions
12 carrot sticks, peeled and cut into 2 inch sections

1. Peel onion's outer skin and cut a small "x" in the root end.
2. Place a steamer basket into a pot with water (water should not touch the steamer basket).
3. Place onions root side down on steamer basket, cover and steam for 15-20 minutes.
4. In a separate pot, steam the carrots for 10-15 minutes. If you do not have another steamer basket, boil the carrots for 5-10 minutes in a covered pan with just enough water to cover.
5. Mix and serve.

Blushing Pears

6 ripe pears, peeled
$\frac{1}{2}$ cup sugar
$1\frac{1}{2}$ quarts cranberry-raspberry juice
1 cinnamon stick
1 cup heavy whipping cream
powdered sugar
vanilla

1. Combine the sugar and the juice in a large saucepan. Heat over medium heat, stirring until the sugar has dissolved. Add the cinnamon stick.

2. Bring the mixture to a gentle boil and add the pears. Poach at a low simmer, turning the pears carefully, until they are easily pierced with a knife, about 20 minutes.
3. Allow the pears to cool in the syrup. Turning them once or twice. When they are cool, drain them and reserve the syrup.
4. Place the syrup over high heat, reduce to about 1 cup. Set aside to cool.
5. Whip the heavy cream until it forms soft peaks. Add 1 teaspoon of vanilla and 3 tablespoons of powdered sugar and whip into stiff peaks.
6. Pour some syrup on each plate first, place the pear on top of it. Put a dollop of whipped cream on the side of each pear and drizzle the remaining syrup over the pears. Serve at once.

Glossary

Here are some cooking terms that may need a little explanation.

Baste	To coat with pan juices or marinade using a brush made for this purpose.
Brown	To cook until a light golden brown color.
Chill	To put in the refrigerator until cool.
Chop	To cut into pieces about $\frac{1}{2}''$ thick.
Core	To cut the seeds, stem, and core out of a fruit.
Cream	To blend together using a spoon until the mixture reaches a creamy or smooth consistency.
Cube	To cut into $\frac{1}{2}''$ cubes.
Dice	To cut into small pieces.
Dredge	To coat with flour.
Dress	To add dressing to a salad and toss lightly.
Drizzle	To pour over a few drops at a time.
Garnish	To decorate before serving.
Grease	To lightly coat with oil, margarine, or butter.
Half and Half	A product which is a combination of half milk and half cream.
Mince	Chopped into very tiny pieces.
Parboil	To plunge food into boiling water for a few minutes.
Pierce	To punch small holes into the pie crust so steam escapes.
Pinch	A small amount taken between the thumb and forefinger.
Poach	To cook in simmering liquid.
Reserve	To save until a later step in the recipe.
Sauté	To cook quickly in butter or oil, stirring constantly.
Sift	To lighten and separate flour or other dry ingredients using a sifter.
Simmer	To cook over low heat; not boiling.
Shortening	Butter, margarine, lard, or Crisco-type product.
Stir fry	To cook quickly in oil in a wok (Chinese style).

Index